Oh, whatever can that be?

This is a place that I don't know,
Although it's where I thought I'd go
When I was young and opened books
For open arms and beating hearts.

The paths are full of butterflies
And flowers that I should recognise;
But nothing is quite as it looks:
Nothing quite ending as it starts.

Oh, whatever can that be?

A book of riddles

Matador
9 De Montfort Mews
Leicester LE1 7FW, UK
Tel: (+44) 116 255 9311 / 9312
Email: books@troubador.co.uk
Web: www.troubador.co.uk/matador

ISBN 978-1906510-626

Mixed Sources
Product group from well-managed
forests and other controlled sources
www.fsc.org Cert no. TT-COC-2082
© 1996 Forest Stewardship Council

Printed in the UK by The Cromwell Press Ltd, Wiltshire, UK

Matador is an imprint of Troubador Publishing Ltd

Bryony Driver
1960-2000

My body's slim, my skin is smooth,
My shoulders catch the light;
I stand up straight and do not move
As I dance through the night.

I toss my head so you can see
And yet I will not stay,
For just as you grow used to me,
My body slips away.

I hide my face, grow pale and thin:
Tonight it seems that I must die;
But look for me in two weeks' time
When my round body rules the sky.

Fast over seas of blue and white,
Swift under skies of white and blue;
I wear these colours as I race
To spend my summer close to you.

I build my house outside your house,
Beneath your roof, high on your wall,
So when my children step outside
They have to fly or else they fall.

High up above, huge pillows spilt
A fall of feathers, soft and light;
And we lay snug beneath its quilt:
All silent, still and gleaming white.

Leaving a dark path,
Five silent creatures
Carry their flying friend
Across a snow white field.

Slugs only live to love me –
Me! –
Who children love to hate.
Strange, then,
How gardeners kill the slugs
And pile me
On children's plates.

Tiny and green
I fell to earth,
Where, in the dark,
You had your birth.

A slender child
In shadowed lands,
Where you once stood
A giant stands.

When I am young
I have more feet,
And crawl across
The food I eat.

When I'm older
I wake one day,
Unfold my wings
And fly away.

Dressed in clothes that no-one wears,
And used last night, though made today,
I bring you peace and frightful dreams:
A place to rest, but not to stay.

When the hottest summer sun beats down
I have a thick green dress I wear;
When the coldest storms of winter blow
I stand in snow, my body bare.

First lay me down on my broad back.
Then, gently, or my spine will crack,
Turn over these white sheets to find
The silent thoughts that speak my mind.

My sister and I – we look alike –
Walk everywhere together;
Bows and eyes and tongues tied tight,
We brave all kinds of weather.

As greedy as a giant,
But smaller than a mouse,
I roam around your garden,
But never leave my house.

I
Am
China.
Indian
Leaves
Arrive.
Hat off,
Belly fills,
Throat spills
In different
China.

I lived in one long silent room
That ran forever through the gloom.
No carpet lay along the floor,
No locks, no windows, keys or door,
And on the day I slipped outside
To breathe in the fresh air; I died.

When darkness falls
On a wintry night,
Close my eyes
To hide the sight.

For while the storm
Roars roundabout
I'm warm within
And wet without.

But when the sun
Shines on the snow,
I'll open wide
To let you go.

Terrified of everybody,
Hiding in the grass,
An orchestra of thousands
Jumps up as you walk past.

Not an instrument between them,
Making music in the sun,
The orchestra of thousands
Stops once the day is done.

Never singing, saying nothing,
Playing summer's simplest song,
The orchestra of thousands
Dies when winter comes along.

She and her sisters work long hours,
To make what no one can:
Soft-scented light and food, from flowers,
The sweetest known to man.

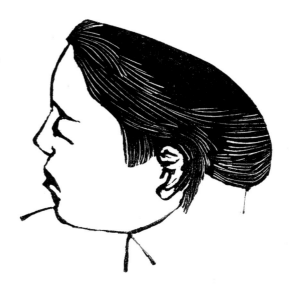

In the Spring, I'm young and pretty,
In Summer, though, I fall apart.
In Autumn, look where I once danced
To find the gift that holds my heart.

It may not grow for years and years:
Yet don't be sad, or dry your eyes.
Water it gently with your tears,
For once it flowers, it never dies.

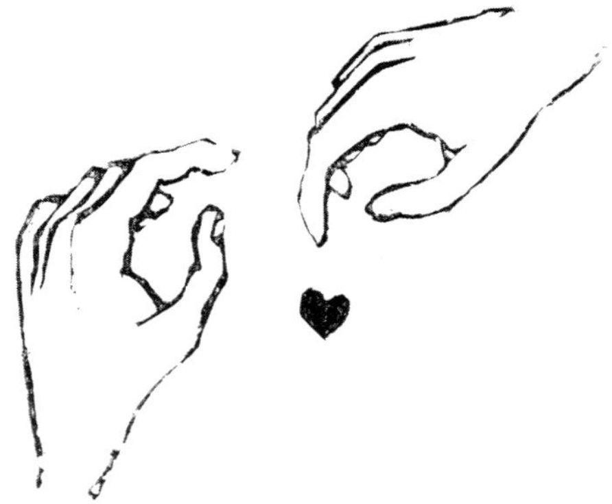